On March 12, 1933, the voice of newly-elected President Franklin Delano Roosevelt crackled across the air waves and into the homes of hundreds of thousands of Americans listening to their radios. Roosevelt explained the banking crisis in hopes that he could ward off a major panic. His voice was calm but firm. "Let me state the simple fact that when you deposit money in a bank the bank does not put the money into a safe deposit vault," he explained. "It invests your money in many different forms of credit — bonds, mortgages. In other words, the bank puts your money to work. Part of the money is kept in currency — sufficient to cover the cash needs of the average citizen.... The total amount of all the currency in the country is only a small fraction of the total deposits in all of the banks.... Because of undermined confidence, there was a general rush to turn bank deposits into currency. On the spur of the moment it was, of course, impossible to sell perfectly sound assets of a bank and convert them into cash except at panic prices far below their real value.

"It was then that I issued the proclamation for the nationwide bank holiday. The second step was the legislation passed by the Congress to extend the holiday and lift the ban of that holiday gradually. This law also gave authority to develop a program of rehabilitation of our banking facilities....

"When the banks resume a very few people who have not recovered from their fear may again begin withdrawals. Let me make clear that the banks will take care of all needs — and it is my belief that when the people find that they can get their money the phantom of fear will soon be laid....

"Confidence and courage are the essentials in our plan. You must have faith; you must not be stampeded by rumors. We have provided the machinery to restore our financial system; it is up to you to support and make it work. Together we cannot fail."

2

# High Times & Hard Times

## OKLAHOMA 1920-1940

**Western National Bank**
**Tulsa, Oklahoma**

Produced for Western National Bank of Tulsa
by The Blakey Group Inc.
ISBN 0-914381-03-2

*Away With Rum*
*Prohibition was a national effort to uplift the morals of the country, to save sinners from themselves. Salvation Army and public officials combined efforts to rid the world of liquor. Joe Hardin/Mildred Hardin Collection.*

4

**Confounding the Enemy**
*During World War I, Choctaw Indians were used to send telephone messages since the Choctaw language could not be decoded by enemy troops. When the men returned from war, they had changed — and so had the towns and the girls they had left behind.
Left to right: Oklahoma Historical Society, Blakey Group Collection.*

```
976.6052 H537 1984
High times & hard times :
Oklahoma, 1920-1940
```

# Running Wild

The war to end all wars had ended in August 1921, and the war-weary soldiers had marched home. They had dreamed of homes and families, jobs and crops and getting ahead in business. Now they faced a new world, and they were eager to get on with living.

There were startling changes. Women now had the vote, and some had even been arrested for smoking. Oklahoma had — perish the thought! — gone Republican for the first time in its history. Coca-Cola was once again five cents a bottle. Hamburger or steak was 15 cents a pound. P&G laundry soap was 25 bars for $1. Kids still followed the ice wagon around, but mostly they saved their pennies for a new treat — Eskimo pies. Health inspectors in small but growing Oklahoma towns tried to outlaw milk cows from city backyards; but mothers protested bitterly that they would not dare poison their children with 'dairy milk.'

The new generation was hooked on entertainment — whether it was movies, vaudeville or opera. The price of the new "airdome" theaters (open on top and sometimes sides) was 20 cents for adults, 10 cents for children. Tom Mix and Pearl White were box office attractions. By the mid-'20s, over a million people a week crowded into movie houses. Charlie Chaplin and Ben Turpin played second fiddle in popularity to Rin-Tin-Tin. Lon Chaney chilled movie-goers in "Phantom of the Opera." Not to be outdone by the movies, one theatre owner presented live vaudeville with 50 midgets, three Shetland ponies and five elephants all performing at once.

6

***Ice-Cold***
*Electricity still had not stretched into the small towns, and ice boxes were still the only way to keep food in the summer. Ice came in 50-pound and 100-pound blocks by the ice man and his horse-drawn wagon.*
*Joe Hardin/Mildred Hardin Collection.*

Women were determined that even hard-bitten oil towns take on the trappings of culture. Some of the more daring read Sinclair Lewis's shocking *Main Street* which had been censored for "creating a distaste for the conventional good life of the American." Okmulgee's Hippodrome Theatre — the largest theater west of the Mississippi with basement swimming pool and velvet box seats — featured such "high-brow" entertainment as Irish tenor John McCormack, Metropolitan Opera Company baritone Renalto Zanelli and pianist Grace Wagner.

For those whose tastes ran to something a little less sedate, the second-floor Hippodrome Amusement Palace included a dance floor mounted on huge springs to create the feeling of dancing on a cloud. More than a thousand persons could trip the light fantastic or dance the Charleston on its surface at one time. By the mid-'20s, ladies were bobbing their hair, and powdered knees showed above rolled-down stockings. People sang such risque songs as "Baby Face," "Ukulele Lady," "Ain't We Got Fun," "Five Foot Two, Eyes of Blue," "If You Knew Susie" and "Runnin' Wild."

An entirely new language was blossoming with the jazz age. "Sex appeal" was a new concept, and plenty of young men found themselves "carrying the torch" for some sweet young thing in a form-fitting bathing suit. There was even a local bathing beauty contest started in Atlantic City — the "Miss America" contest. It was a new youth; and to the older generation — and to themselves — they seemed less innocent than ever before — or at least they liked to believe they were.

8

**Big-City Airs**
*The Scottish game of golf was growing popular at the newly built country clubs. When Empire Oil (later Cities Service) held its annual picnic, executives and office staff tried their hand at it.*
*Cities Service Oil and Gas Corporation Collection.*

For all the talk of jazz babies and flappers, Oklahoma was filled with good solid souls who read their Bibles or their Torahs faithfully. Some were horrified when teachers actually began mentioning the strange theories of Nobel Prizewinner Albert Einstein (What did $E=MC^2$ really mean?) and Charles Darwin (Did man really evolve from monkeys?). When John Scopes was accused of defying Tennessee's state law against teaching evolution in 1925, they read every word of the reports of the "Monkey Trial." Here was a trial of wry wit and wisdom — Clarence Darrow pitted against fundamentalist William Jennings Bryan. Darrow called it "the first trial of its kind since we stopped trying people for witchcraft." But emotion — or God, depending on the point of view — won out. Scopes was found guilty and fined $100.

Golf was popular as country clubs sprang up in small towns. Waistlines on fashionable dresses dropped to the hips. Pocket flasks were popular, and it was even whispered that some ladies carried tiny purse flasks to sip their personal favorite. Oklahomans read about speakeasies in the papers, but they usually confined themselves to buying booze from the local bootlegger. There was still plenty of white lightning being brewed in the hills by those who had put up batches for years. Newer hands occasionally got careless, and a bad batch sometimes resulted in a funeral or two. One county newspaper in 1921 headlined 15 people who had passed on to their maker by imbibing a bad batch of brew.

10

> **Black Mark in History**
> *In 1921, Tulsa broke out in what was then the worst race riot of the century. The fires wiped out Greenwood, then known as the Black Wall Street of America. No one ever knew for sure just how many blacks or whites were killed.*
> Tulsa Chamber of Commerce.

# Men in white sheets

There were more than a dozen black communities at statehood; but their dream of a black state had died. Many blacks moved into urban areas to work. North of Tulsa, one strong black community — Greenwood — grew rapidly. Greenwood blacks not only owned their own businesses, catering to their community; they owned the land and the buildings — uncommon in that day and age. Nicknamed the Black Wall Street of America, the area was almost a national black shrine and a true example of black enterprise.

As both Tulsa and Greenwood began to grow, they were separated only by a strip area which catered to all colors. Hooch joints served a brew known as "Choc" beer, which flowed freely at all hours as did the morals and the mayhem. There was bound to be trouble. It erupted in the summer heat of 1921. The details were clouded — and remained so despite investigations. When the flames and gunshots died down, the results were evident: the Greenwood area had been burned to the ground. At least 70 blacks and 10 whites died — no one was really sure about the numbers. Millions of dollars were lost in homes and businesses that would never be rebuilt. Some black families migrated to nearby towns without looking back. Sympathetic whites hid their maids and gardeners when law enforcement authorities slapped a curfew on blacks. Uneasiness ruled for months. The disaster would go down as the worst race riot in history.

The Tulsa confrontation may have been egged on by the Ku Klux Klan. Certainly the KKK was growing bolder. Pronouncements and photographs appeared in Oklahoma papers — the klan presenting gifts to the Red Cross as to well as widows and orphans. When the Knights of Columbus held anti-klan meetings, fights erupted. Many who opposed the KKK were beaten or shot. Some law officials were plainly on the klan side.

12

*Dinner in the Diner*
*For many years, one of Tulsa's most well-known eating spots was Bishop's Kansas City Waffle House, much favored by downtown office workers for its good food at reasonable prices. Ted Rodgers/Tulsa Chamber of Commerce.*

Governor Jack Walton was determined to clean matters up and took drastic measures. During summer and fall, martial law was declared in parts of Oklahoma, including Oklahoma, Okmulgee and Tulsa counties. Many felt Walton overstepped his bounds. Even though the cause might be worthwhile, his methods were high-handed. In September, Walton suspended the writ of habeas corpus in Tulsa and ordered his militia to collect the arms of citizens. When an outcry arose, he threatened to put the entire state under martial law. N.C. Jewett, grand dragon of the state klan, charged sour grapes — that Walton was vindictive because he had tried to join the klan but had been blackballed. Walton ordered an automatic martial law status for any area "where masked men parade or appear." He placed a military censor in the *Tulsa Tribune* office and threatened the same in Muskogee and Oklahoma City. He promised to jail legislators if they tried to convene. On September 16, the day before an Oklahoma County grand jury was to investigate his activities, he declared statewide martial law. Oklahoma hit the national news as Walton indicted the state for rebellion, riot and insurrection. "Governor Walton cannot suspend the constitution," wrote one editor. "He has no more right to suspend the privileges of citizenship written in the very basic law of this commonwealth, than masked men have to inflict penalty with a split strap."

As the governor ordered a military court of inquiry and issued "shoot-to-kill" orders to the National Guard to prevent the legislature from assembling at the capitol, klan membership swelled. Another editor wrote that the governor's actions were actually making the KKK downright respectable. Although Walton tried to halt a special election for constitutional revisions, the election was held and Walton was formally ousted from office.

14

*A Horse for Companion*
*Eddie Burgess was a popular Oklahoma cowboy who made the rodeo circuit. In bad times, he bedded down with his horse on the train.*
*Okmulgee Public Library.*

# Heroes and Heroines

Rodeos were just beginning to catch on in the East, and everyone read about Oklahoma's own cowboy-humorist Will Rogers visiting Europe as President Calvin Coolidge's Ambassador of Good Will. Another Oklahoma cowboy popular in the early '20s was Eddie Burgess, a full-blood Creek Indian. Burgess, his brother Riley and two cousins set out on the rodeo circuit. When times were flush, they made good money. When they could not afford a Pullman berth on the train, Eddie simply bedded down with his horse in the cattle car. On July 25, 1923, while competing in a rodeo at Cheyenne, a rope broke, and the horse fell backwards. Eddie was pinned underneath, the saddle horn landed on his skull. He died a few hours later.

Oklahoma's four-legged sports figures were also drawing attention. Tulsa horses finished first and second in the Kentucky Derby in May 1923. In the spring of 1924, Tulsa's own Black Gold won the Kentucky Derby.

Hundreds cheered as 19-year-old Gertrude Ederle swam the English Channel. Everyone rooted for baseball's Babe Ruth, (he hit his 60th home run in 1926). Local baseball teams in smaller towns took their games to heart and were not above finishing a match with fists. In 1927, Charles A. Lindbergh took off from Roosevelt Field in a small plane, and 33 1/2 hours later landed in Paris.

Then there was Andy Payne. Andy Payne was 19, a curly-headed Indian youth who had grown up west of Foyil. In 1928, he entered the first International Transcontinental Foot Marathon, better known as the Bunion Derby. Payne had had to run to and from school to get daily chores done and felt confident he could make it. He wanted to win enough money to bail out his father's mortgaged farm. Over 300 eager young men started the race in Los Angeles on February 13. By May 5, what was left of them — about 70 — had reached Chicago. When a weary and footsore Payne trotted into Madison Square Garden 3,424 miles and 86 days later, there were only 54 others behind him. He had made the 3,422.3 miles in 573 hours, four minutes and 34 seconds — an average of six miles an hour. He had lost 20 pounds but gained $25,000 — more than enough to pay off his father's mortgage.

A Miner at his Task
Henryetta, Okla.
(Nardin)

**Dark in the Mine**
*Coal mining was still the major source of energy and big business in the state. Oklahoma miners represented all nationalities — Poles, Italians, Swedes, Lithuanians as well as other European stock.*
*Joe Hardin/Mildred Hardin Collection.*

# THE BUSINESS OF AMERICA

Coal was a major industry in eastern Oklahoma; and miners had been brought in from the north and east. The population of the mining towns included English, Scottish, Italian, Polish, French, Yugoslav and Mexican miners with a handful of Syrian, Jewish and Lebanese merchants.

Coolidge had declared that the "business of America is business," and everyone seemed to agree. America was ready to buy — and buy and they did even when they had no money. Installment payments quintupled, accounting for 90 percent of all purchases of pianos, sewing and washing machines, 80 percent of the vacuum cleaners, radios and refrigerators, 70 percent of all furniture and 60 percent of all automobiles.

Prices were cheap by today's standards. A washing machine averaged $97.50, a phonograph $43.50, a refrigerator $87.50, a vacuum cleaner $28.95. Haircuts were 35 cents, shaves 15 cents at most barbershops.

Tulsans swore their city's population exceeded Oklahoma City's in July 1924. The familiar "number please" voice disappeared as dial telephones were installed in major metropolitan areas.

There was another new trend in business — the chain store. S.S. Kresge, Lerner Shops, Western Auto Supply, F.W. Woolworth, Skaggs, Safeway — they were all growing on the wave of another new phenomena known as advertising. Honeyed phrases sold everything from Lucky Strikes to Holeproof Hosiery. Some called it pure schmaltz, but sales catapulted. Burma-Shave's plain signs by the side of the road with their quaint phrases saved one family company from bankruptcy.

The automobile was the ultimate symbol of American industry and growth. For the wealthy, it was easy to indulge in a Stutz Bearcat, Pierce-Arrow, Lincoln, Cadillac Phaeton or Packard Runabout with rumble seat. An imported Mercedes started at a mere $21,500. Those with limited budgets could always get a Ford Model T — $290 f.o.b. Detroit — and plenty of them did. Every second car on the road was a Ford. Garages sprang up everywhere, and Tulsa's last livery stable went out of business. Battery stations rented batteries for 25 cents a day while old batteries were recharged or rebuilt for only $1 (and up).

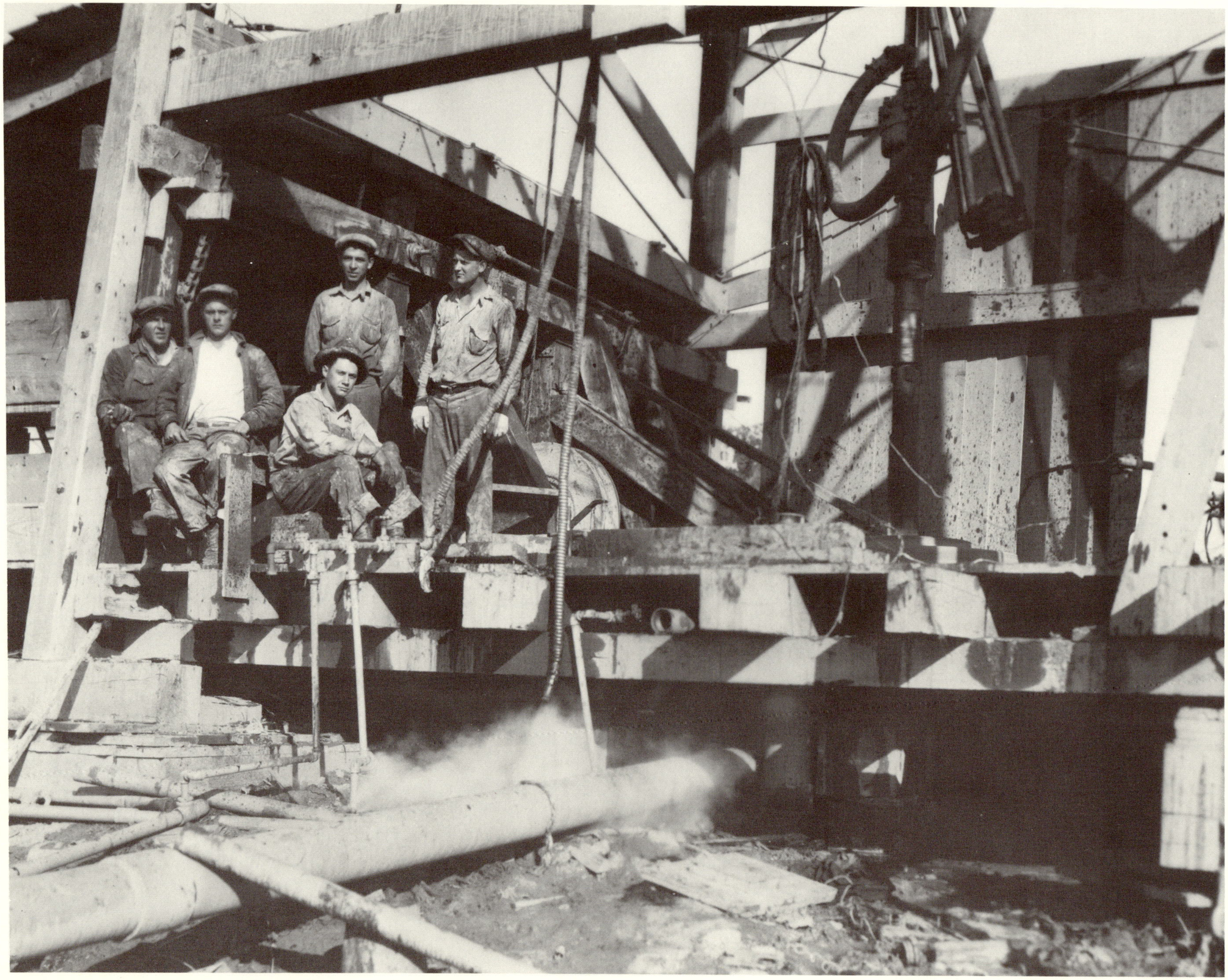

*Working in the Field*
*Oil field workers were paid good wages, and plenty of farm boys deserted the wheat and cotton fields for the oil field. The Seminole oil field came in with such a boom that prices dropped to the bottom of the barrel.*
*Cities Service Oil and Gas Corporation Collection.*

# Red Man in a White Man's World

Oil was the bright jewel in the state's crown. Osage County, Glennpool and the Tonkawa field were going great guns. Okmulgee County alone produced 40,000 barrels of oil a day. It was a heady figure when oil was selling for $4 a barrel. People drilled wherever they thought they might strike a well. Fever was so frenzied that if the only bare spot a man owned was his backyard, he was apt to drill that. When the Seminole oil field came in, production was so heavy that prices dropped severely. The Oklahoma City field, which exploded in 1928, made matters worse. There really could be too much of a good thing. In 1929, the Oklahoma Corporation Commission ordered a 30-day shutdown of the Oklahoma City field because of wasteful overproduction, and stricter conservation laws were enacted.

Oil catapulted the Oklahoma Indian into the twentieth century whether he wanted to be or not. The crafty Osage had maintained their tribal identity and kept their mineral rights with the tribe. As a result, when the dollars were doled out among the heirs, even the poorest tribesmen were suddenly wealthy. Some tribes had divided up mineral rights to the individuals when the power of the tribes had been broken. That made it simple for unscrupulous men to purchase a single plot of land and its mineral rights.

20

**Gumbo Alley**
*The Seminole field was notorious for crowded streets as oil companies and oil equipment suppliers moved in. When it rained, the soil composition turned to gumbo, and everything came to a halt as people pushed and shoved their horses, mules and vehicles through the ensuing mess.*
*Blakey Group Collection.*

Another easy way to get at the Indian's fortune was to question his intelligence, as happened in the case of Creek Indian Jackson Barnett. Since Barnett spoke no English, no one was sure just how much he really understood about the white man's laws or his money. The truth was, Barnett probably cared very little about either. When oil was discovered on his property, his daily income jumped to between $5,000 and $14,000, depending on who was passing the story along. Barnett allowed much of it to be given away — to churches and other charitable causes. His white guardians saw to it that he had enough pocket money to hold modest feasts or give small amounts to friends. Then Anna Laura Lowe, a white divorcee, drove into his life, spirited him away to Kansas where they were married and on to Missouri where a second ceremony was performed. From that time on, Barnett was in the news as the guardians, government and wife fought over him. Anna moved him to Los Angeles where she built an 18-room colonial home. No one could really prove she was only after his money, and no one could charge her with neglect. She changed Barnett from a barefoot Indian into a dapper millionaire whose complexion was powdered with diamond dust. Barnett, however, remained simple at heart and was often seen near his Los Angeles mansion, dressed in a policeman's uniform, directing traffic. The court battles that ensued over his wealth and the would-be heirs dragged on until after his death.

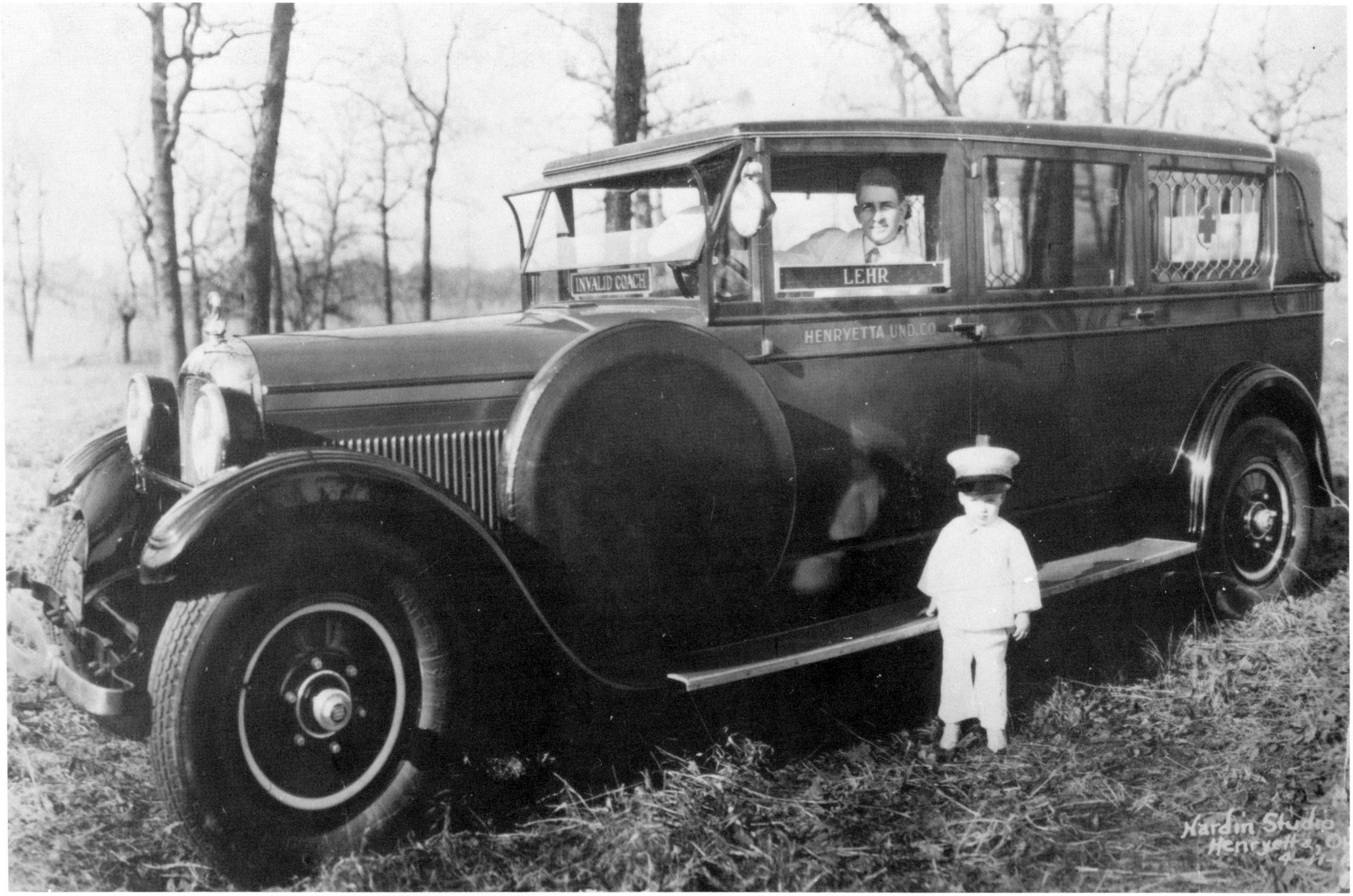
INVALID COACH
LEHR
HENRYETTA UND. CO.
Nardin Studio

***Leaded Glass for the Ill***
*Leaded glass windows marked Lehr's "Invalid Coach." Lehr's small son went along for the ride in an ambulance outfit made by his mother.*
*Joe Hardin/Mildred Hardin Collection.*

Katie Fixico was a young Indian orphan and ward of her tribe. Like Barnett, she was declared incompetent and her financial affairs turned over to a white guardian. Katie owned nearly a dozen homes in Oklahoma, each furnished with full-time servants. Generous to a fault, she often bought an entire truckload of cakes or pies for a church gathering or worthwhile society. Her parties often lasted weeks; and if a guest decided to leave before she thought appropriate, she simply shot out the automobile tires. They were replaced when she felt the time to leave was right. If one of her Rolls Royces or Pierce Arrows ran out of fuel or developed a minor problem, she was apt to simply discard it.

Such Indians had little concept of how much money the guardians managed to pocket privately. Those who did know felt the guardians were charging enormous fees totally out of proportion to their duties. The Creek Council drew up a formal protest against guardians and others preying on Indian estates. The complaint was heard before the Secretary of the Interior and the Attorney General of the United States. Eight guardians were indicted and a number of county officials were suspended from office. But the Supreme Court eventually reinstated every one. It was one more bitter pill for the Indian to swallow.

24

***Herding Buffalo on the 101 Ranch***
*The fame of the Miller Brothers 101 Ranch near Ponca City was spread through its wild west show which toured the country. A model outfit, it employed every new technique and tool possible. It was said that when you sat down to a meal, everything but the olives had been grown on the ranch.*
*Oklahoma State Historical Society.*

# Chickens and Velvet Slippers

In 1928, Republicans were preaching "two chickens in every pot and two cars in every garage." Herbert Hoover won the presidential election; but it was rumored that Calvin Coolidge had predicted a depression and refused to accept nomination because of it. Naturally, that had to be nonsense. Everyone was doing splendidly. Millionaires in Oklahoma City, as one editor pointed out, walked on brussels, wore velvet slippers, silk underwear and diamond rings.

Of course, there were others who did not seem so well off. The Nuyaka Indian Mission school burned to the ground. Workers were organizing for better wages and better working conditions. In the mining towns, families burned dead car batteries for heat in winter and counted themselves lucky to have running water. Most were eternally in debt to the company stores. When trouble broke out in the Henryetta mines, hundreds of families from Arkansas and Oklahoma mining communities drove into the area to support the strikers. National Guardsmen aggravated the situation, and fighting broke out. Troops were finally withdrawn, and miners returned to work without union recognition. In June 1929, Oklahoma Union Railway Employees fared better. They were granted a three-cent raise in wages after a two-week labor dispute.

There were rumors of trouble on the stock market, but most people believed it would straighten itself out. Even when the stock market took a drastic dive on October 29, 1929, few wanted to think such a thing could happen — much less last very long. But there were too many people in debt on margin, and as stockbrokers called the margins, too few could come up with the cash. The paper house collapsed. On November 2, over 12 million shares were dumped on the market. Securities fell $40 billion in the next few weeks.

The stock market crash brought down hundreds of small businessmen — and some larger ones, such as the Miller Brothers 101 Ranch near Ponca City. The ranch had become a national institution, a model self-sufficient farm, where everything from beef to wheat was raised. Its hospitality was legendary, and its Wild West Show toured throughout the world, complete with such characters as Bill Pickett, a black man who bulldogged steers by his teeth.

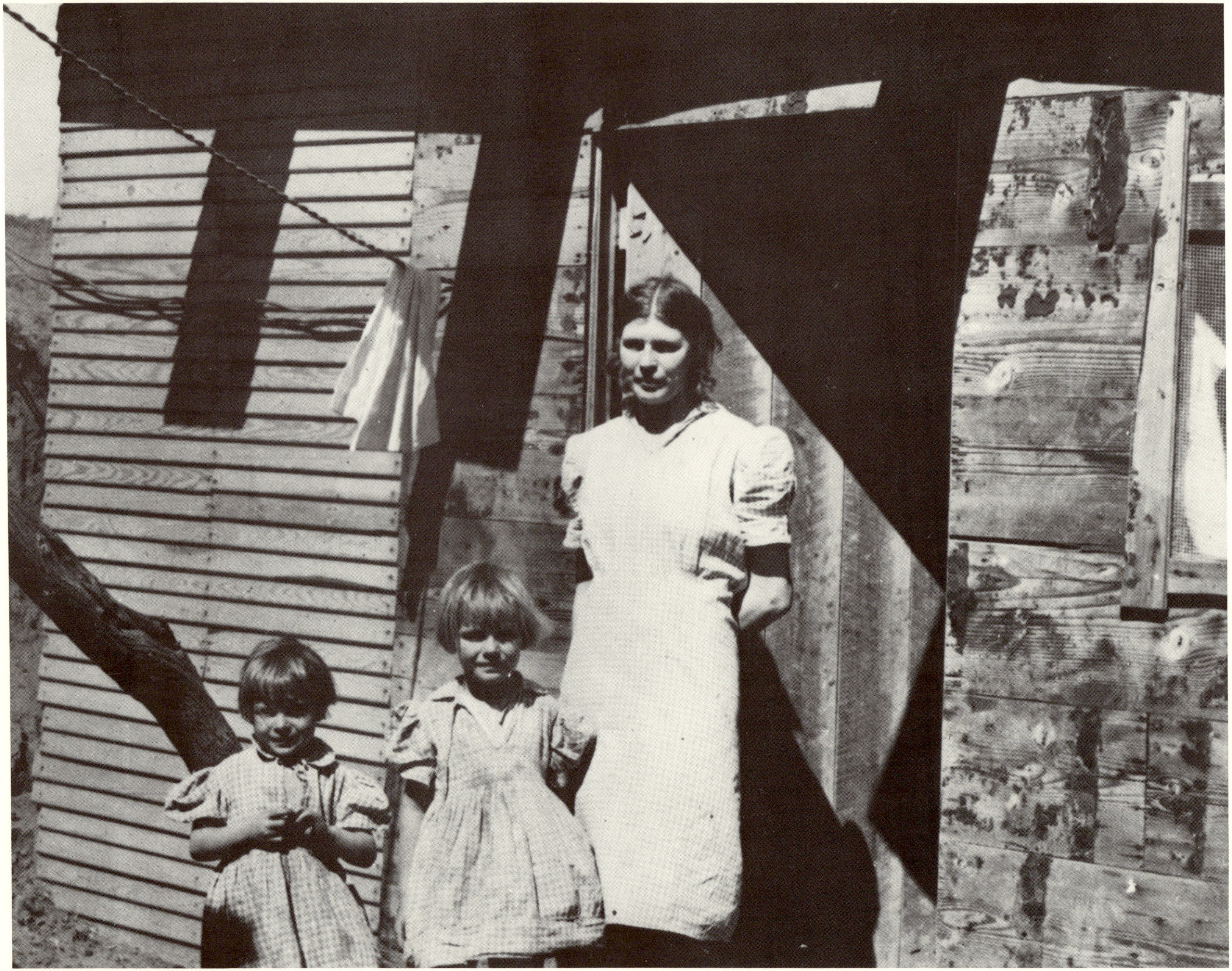

*Faces of Poverty*
*With no rain and the topsoil gone with the dust storms, farmers were left with little but their mortgages. The desperation crept across even the youngest faces. Those who left often struck out with nothing but a mattress or two, the clothes on their back and a few dollars in their pocket. When Dorothea Lange photographed one young woman going west, she noted, "They had been living on [unmarketable] vegetables and birds that the children killed. She had just sold the tires from her car to buy food."*
*Library of Congress.*

# A LONG HARD WEATHER

In 1930, Oklahoma's population was 2,396,040. After 12 years of work, U.S. 77 was completed; it was the first paved road that went all the way across the state. The economic picture was glum everywhere, and the weather didn't seem to help. In January, temperatures fell below zero and kept on going. On January 22, after weeks of snow and sleet, the thermometer dropped to 18 below zero.

Unemployment soared. President Hoover Hoover announced, "I am convinced we have passed the worst and with continued effort we will rapidly recover." But three million Americans were out of work. Those who had steady jobs were glad to get them. Few balked at what they were asked to do. For every job, a hundred waited outside. Frisco railroad workers earned 32 cents an hour. At Reda Pump in Bartlesville workers were paid 40 cents an hour. Bank tellers often kept books, operated a handcranked Burroughs, worked in a teller window and swept the floor after the bank closed.

27

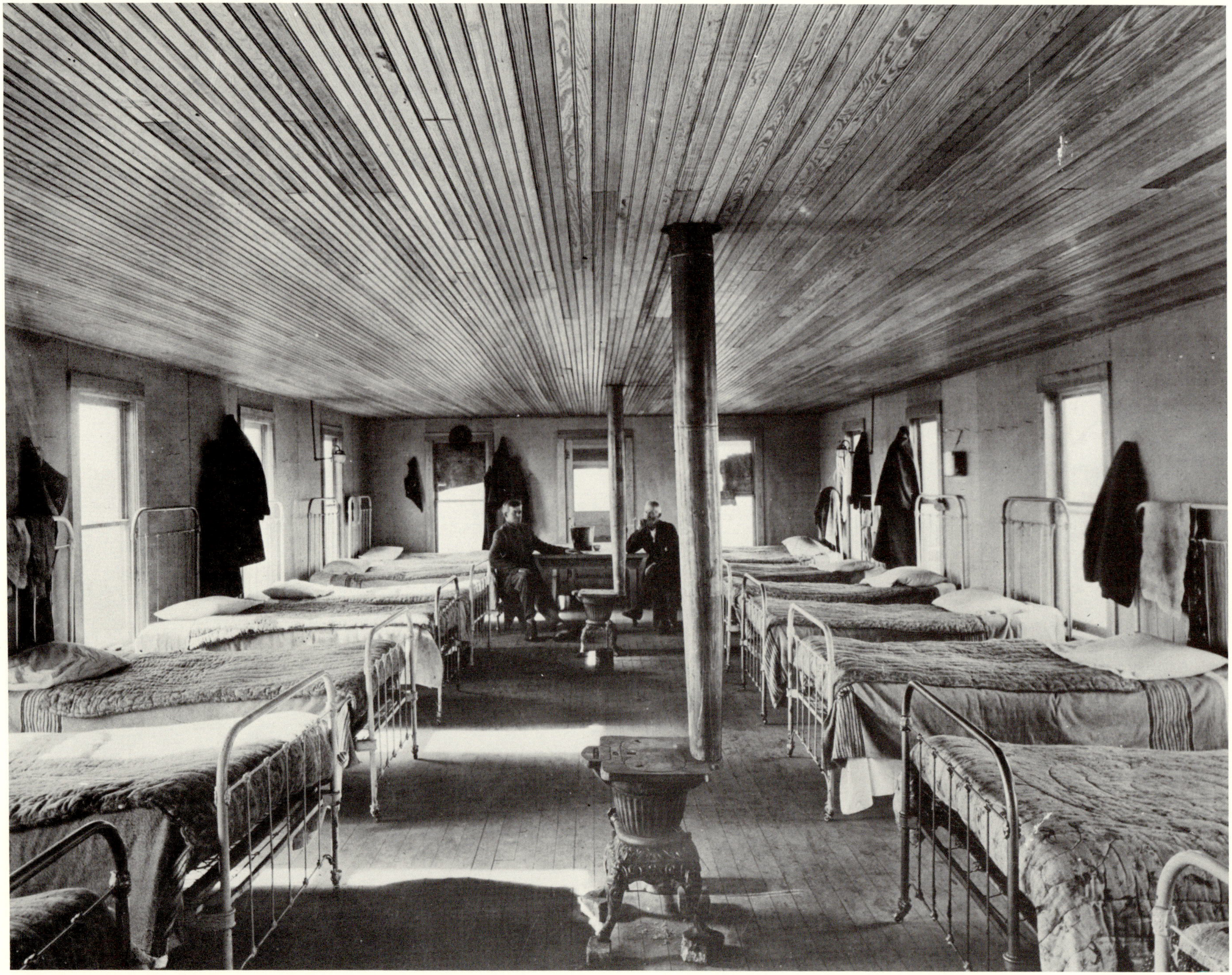

**The Bunkhouse**
*The search for oil in Oklahoma was a 24-hour-a-day job. That often meant living on the site. Two roughnecks take a break in the bunkhouse. Beryl Ford Collection.*

Surely prosperity was just around the corner; everyone said so. But everyone was wrong. By summer, Oklahoma's land was drier than anyone remembered. The ground cracked open as temperatures soared to 107 degrees. To make matters worse, a bushel of corn dropped to 25 cents, a bale of cotton to $25. No farmer could live on that income. President Hoover formed the Farm Bureau in an effort to shore up wheat and cotton prices. Will Rogers held entertainments for drought relief. Peanuts were introduced as an alternate crop for Oklahoma farmers, but an onslaught of heavy rains ruined the harvest. For the most part, crops just dried up even more. Experts at the state agricultural college at Stillwater held meetings to discuss how to increase production by terracing, crop rotation and soil analysis. A stay-out-of-debt program was set up for wives of black farmers, and the home demonstration agent taught canning, sewing and general housework. More farm women took to canning whatever had managed to survive the drought. When cows were too expensive to feed, many turned to the stocky little goat. The prolific rabbit was nicknamed the "Hoover hog."

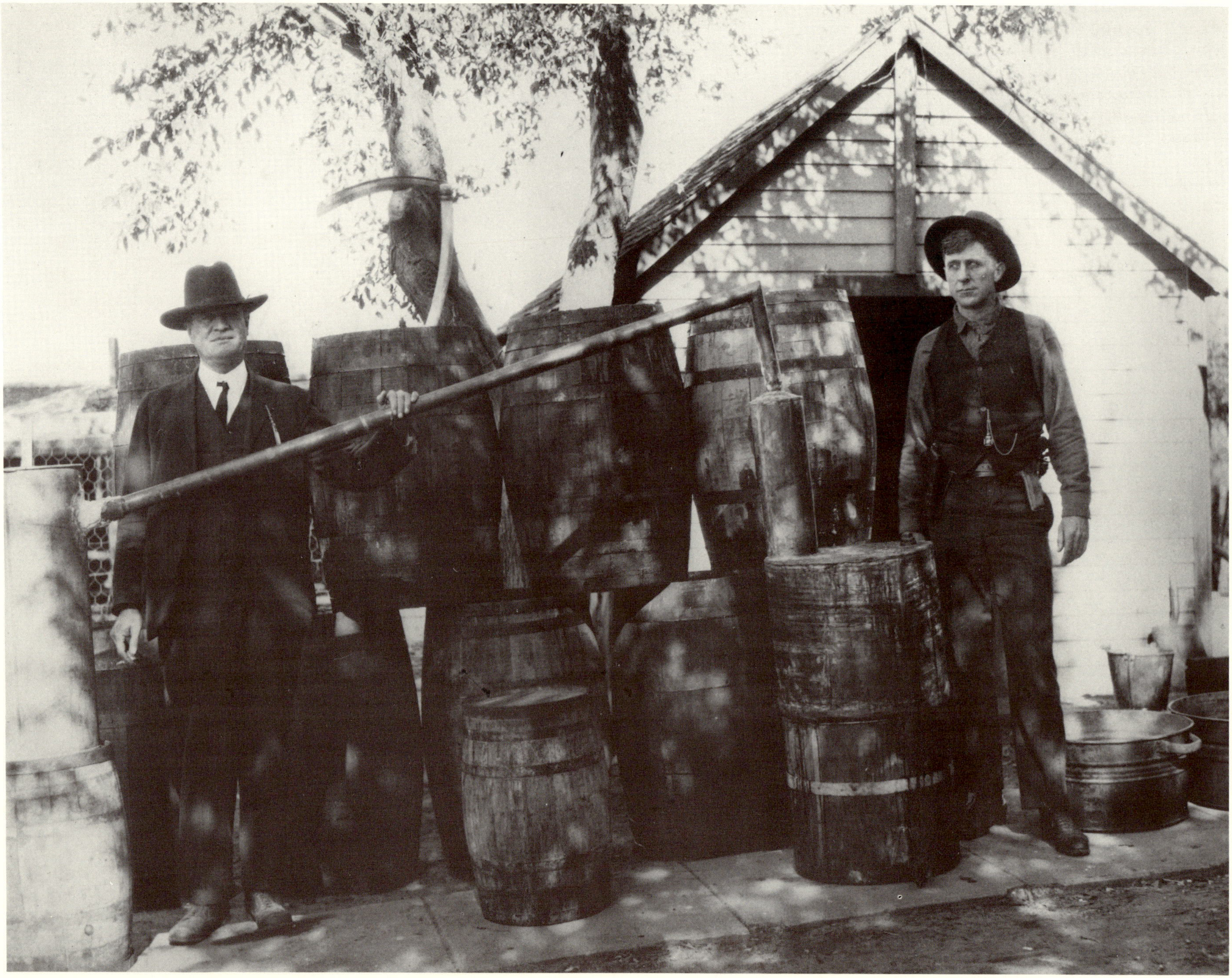

*Hi, Mom*
*Oil field kids kept occupied with their own brand of fun on this homemade derrick. Cities Service Oil and Gas Corporation Collection.*

In Oklahoma, banks were suffering as the state's biggest industries — agriculture and oil — started a downhill slide. Oil profits were drying up as badly as the farmlands. For years, the bankers had depended on repayment of loans from annual crops. But nothing was growing. For years, the more daring had bankrolled wildcatters in the oil fields. They loaned to those who ran the businesses which drilled the wells and laid the pipelines and hauled the equipment. Now even though oil was coming out of the ground, it was not paying the bills as it had before.

Of Henryetta's six banks, only Central National Bank remained open and then simply because one oil man was determined that it remain open and had the money to keep it afloat. Other banks without such liquid investors had few choices. The effect upon the entire Oklahoma economy was devastating. Bankers could not collect what the people did not have. But like any business, they too had obligations — salaries, bills, investors. The banker was often left with two choices: he could foreclose on the mortgages and loans by taking collateral that no one — not even the bank — really wanted; or he could close the bank. It often depended upon the banker's own heart which path he pursued. It was a toss of a coin, and either way, he was doomed.

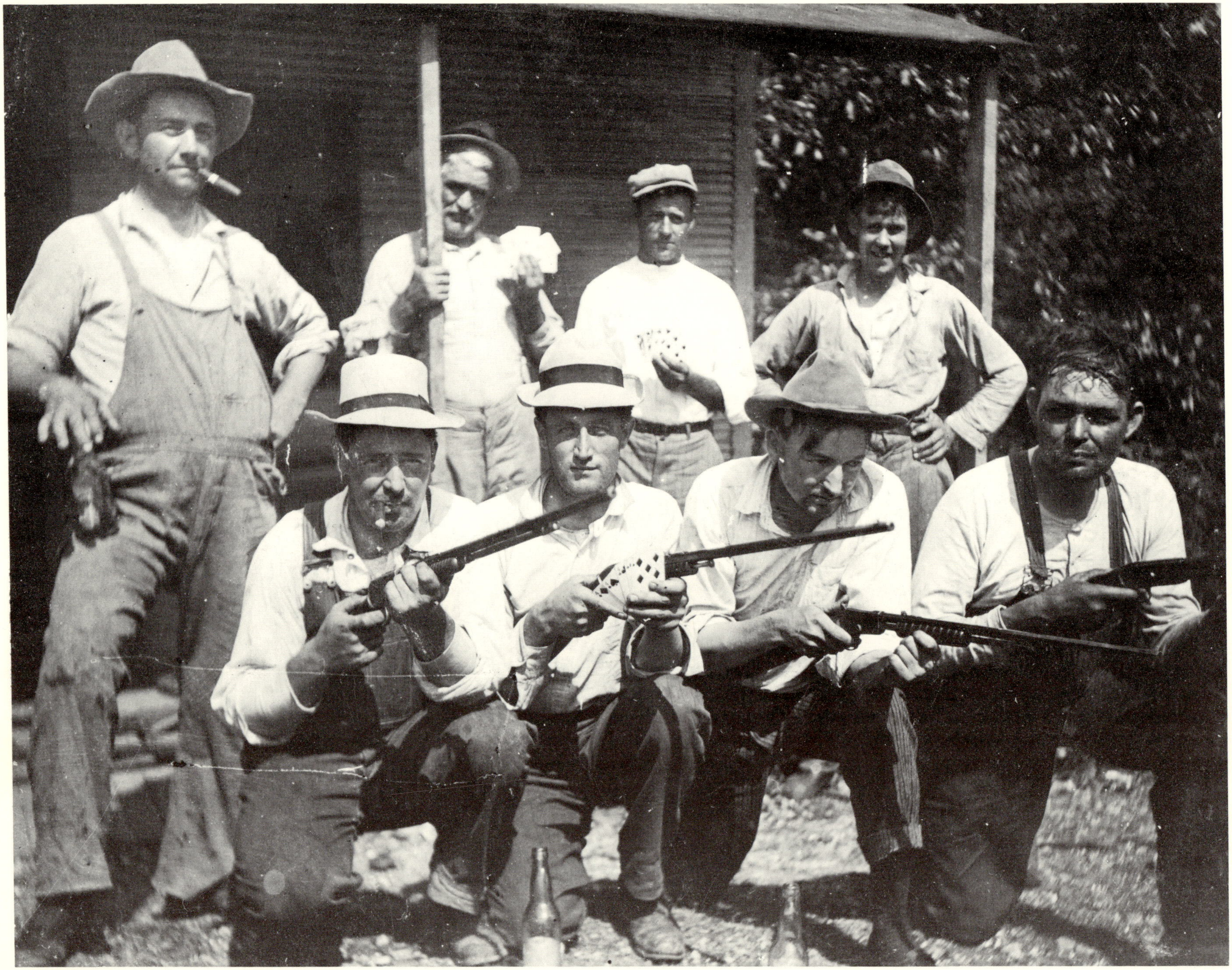

*Ever Ready*
*Cookson Hills folk might pose for a picture in jest, but a lawman who asked too many questions about home brew or bandits was liable to find himself facing the wrong end of the gun barrel.*
*Blakey Group Collection.*

# Outcasts and Outlaws

The people who had settled Oklahoma only a decade or two before were largely those who had nothing to lose and everything to gain in a move West. It seemed to them that there was something unfair about the banks foreclosing on farmers who had struggled so hard to stay alive. But it also seemed unfair when the banks closed their doors and left depositors without their hard-earned dollars. These sons and daughters of society's outcasts were not about to sit still when they felt they were being wronged. A new generation of outlaws struck out against the helplessness of their families and neighbors caught in the cruel weather and the unforeseen economic circumstances.

Bank robberies had never actually ended from the early days although they had been less frequent after statehood. Capitol Hill Bank in one of Oklahoma City's exclusive neighborhoods had been robbed in the mid-'20s. In the late '20s, Matthew Kimes and his gang probably robbed the First National Bank of Kaw City and Farmers State Bank at Burbank. No sooner had they been captured and released, than they hit Farmers National Bank in Beggs, Depew State Bank and Sapulpa State Bank. The small town of Beggs seemed like easy pickings, and Kimes decided to hit three banks — Farmers National, First National and American National — all at the same time. But the robbery did not go as planned when the town clock (by which all activities were paced) developed problems. They netted a mere $18,000, the law close behind as they escaped across state lines. A few months later, Kimes was captured at the Grand Canyon, returned to Oklahoma and sentenced to prison.

WILSON'S
SHOE REPAIR
SHOP No 2
SHOES REBUILT
WHILE YOU WAIT
HOTEL
BUICK HOTEL
DRUGS
BARBEC
SANDWICH
No 9-P

*Traffic, Tulsa Style*
*The oil boom made Tulsa a bustling metropolis within a few short years. Its people came from all directions and all walks of life. This scene at 3rd and Boulder Ave. depicts a city sophisticated enough to boast a neo-Classic courthouse, yet down-home enough to include a barbeque stand. Sixty years later, the courthouse still stands as a federal office building. And Tulsans still like their barbeque. Special Collections, McFarlin Library, University of Tulsa.*

Oklahoma added more than her share to the 1930's roll-call of most-wanted desperadoes. It was said that Charles Arthur (Pretty Boy) Floyd got his start because a Sallisaw bank in which he had had money went bust. Then there were George (Machine Gun) Kelly, Albert L. Bates, Harvey Bailey, Ma Barker and her boys, Alvin Karpis, Bonnie Parker and Clyde Barrow.

Eastern Oklahoma's Cookson Hills was a perfect territory for hiding from the law. There was little cooperation between state and local law officials. Federal law enforcement had yet to be fully organized. Many common folk, dissolutioned by economic circumstances, applauded the bank robbers for "getting even." It was easy to keep the people on the side of the outlaws. Pretty Boy Floyd became the Robin Hood of the Cookson Hills for his small kindnesses. A $20 bill under a dinner plate meant food on the table for a month, and a man was not likely to say much about what he really did not know for sure anyway. Oklahoma's hard-traveling troubadour Woody Guthrie once claimed that there was never an Oklahoma governor half as popular as Pretty Boy. In fact, down in Okemah, where Guthrie came from, it was better not to say much against any of the outlaws. "Something was liable to hit you, son," Guthrie warned, "and it wouldn't be no train."

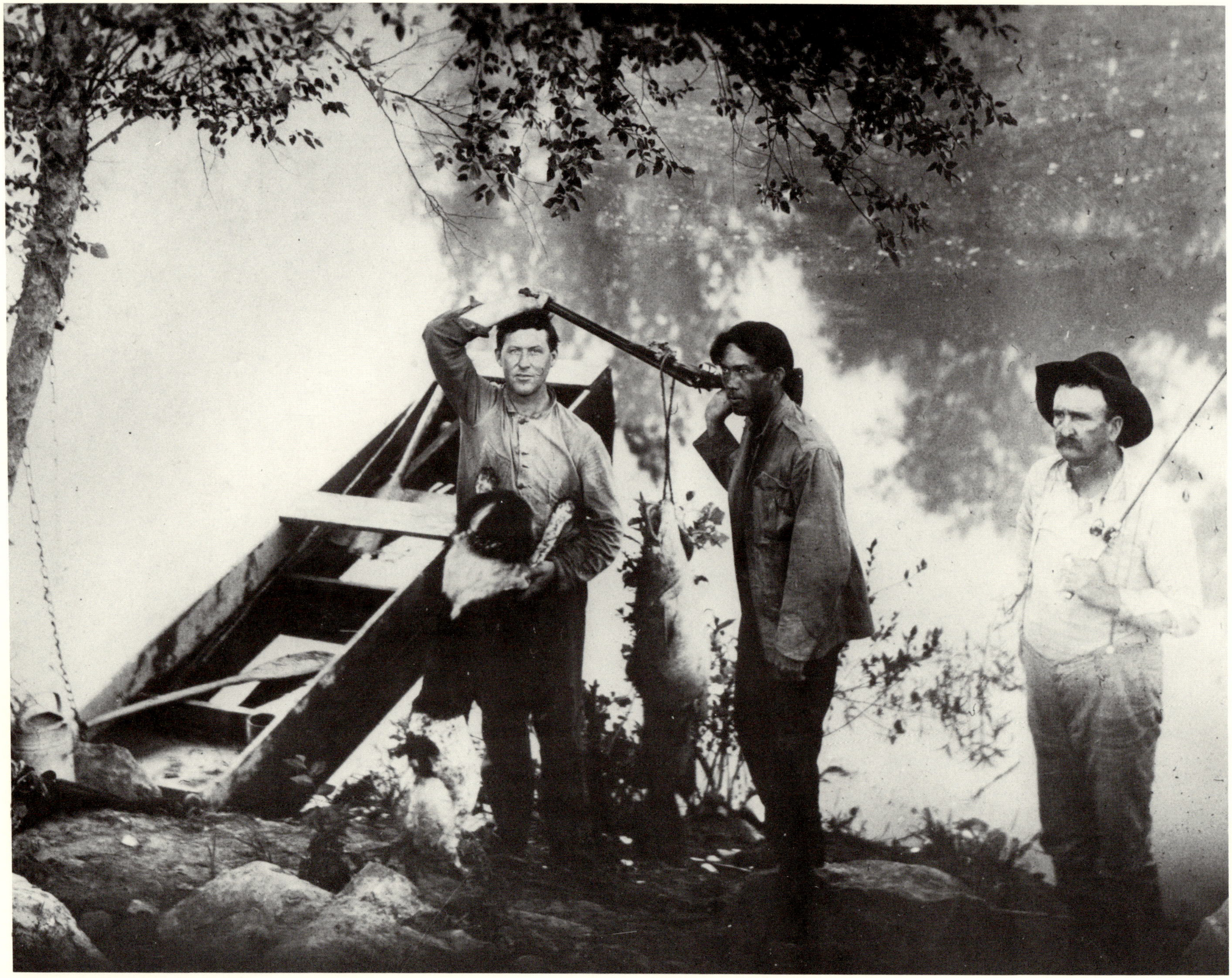

*Gone Fishing*
*Despite the drought and the hard times, there was always time for a little recreation at the fishing hole.*
Oklahoma State Historical Society.

As the Depression dug in to stay, robberies grew more frequent. Morris State Bank was struck twice in 1931. When robbers tried again in May 1932, citizens were waiting. One of the robbers was killed; another was captured and sentenced to 25 years' imprisonment.

Perhaps bank robbery was an easily acquired taste. Before long, Floyd had taken it up fairly regularly. He was a dead shot, and the sheriffs all knew it. Floyd was not above calling the law to notify them when he intended to rob a bank. Usually the sheriff would notice that it was a good day to go fishing and would conveniently be elsewhere for the occasion. Pretty Boy would roar into town, right on time, driving a car loaded with sub-machine guns without much opposition. His escapades kept bankers so nervous that state bank insurance rates doubled one year.

Even when Floyd holed up in town and neighbors knew who he was, most said nothing. Some were afraid; others felt it was none of their business. Floyd was in and out of Tulsa in 1932, taking spurts of visiting and living with his family, even attending movies. When the police finally raided his house, he managed to get away by running between the laundry hanging on the clothesline.

His disappearance did not stop the bank robberies, however. On November 7, 1932, three local bandits robbed the American Exchange Bank of Okmulgee of $11,000. One suspect was caught; but since no one could positively identify him, he was acquitted.

42

***Henryetta Smelter Workers***
*Smelters grew up near Oklahoma's mining areas and provided work for those who preferred to stay above-ground.*
*Joe Hardin/Mildred Hardin Collection.*

In 1933, Machine Gun Kelly kidnapped wealthy Oklahoma City oilman Charles F. Urschel and held him for $200,000 ransom. When the ransom was delivered, Urschel was let go. But J. Edgar Hoover, the new director of the FBI, was determined to make Kelly an example. Some said Hoover was doubly determined because his job was at stake. Whatever his reasons, he dogged Kelly's steps until he captured him in Memphis in 1933. Kelly supposedly cried out, "Don't shoot G-men!" and the name stuck.

Bonnie Parker may have been a lady bank robber but she was certainly no lady. In Atoka, she nagged her new friend, Clyde Barrow, into shooting a sheriff who was about to arrest them for drunk and disorderly conduct. In Oklahoma City, they pulled their car up beside a young policeman directing traffic, asked for directions, then shot the policeman point-blank in the face. John Dillinger once claimed that Bonnie and Clyde were gun-happy punks who "just give bank robbing a bad name." Bonnie and Clyde kept moving — across Texas and Arkansas, getting blamed for a number of jobs they never pulled until they were finally killed in a gun battle in Louisiana May 1934.

Ma Barker, her sons and assorted hangers-on lived in Tulsa during the '20s. The Barker shack on North Cincinnati was an underworld post office and meeting place from which Ma ruled with an iron hand. Her sons — Loyd (Red), Fred, Herman and Arthur (Doc) — were members of the Central Park mob which had at one time 22 hijackers, bandits and other thugs in their ranks. Both Fred and Doc rose to the ranks of Public Enemy No. 1. Ma Barker was killed in Florida in 1935.

44

***Bare-Armed Beauty***
*Bare arms and bare knees marked the bathing beauties of the day. Women were more exercise conscious than ever and sported knickers and sensible walking shoes for hiking.*
*Blakey Group Collection.*

# Dry hopes, dry land

In 1932, nearly one out of every four people in the work force was out of a job. During the summer, an army of jobless World War I veterans — the Bonus Expeditionary Force — marched on Washington to demand their bonus. Army troops turned on them and cleared their crude huts from Anacostia Flats. Farmers took a lesson from the unions. At foreclosure sales, they often threatened auctioneers and conspired to thwart them. Neighbors would get together, bid one or two dollars for an entire farm and furniture, then return it to the farmer about to be dispossessed.

Businesses were still hanging on. Most food which was consumed in the small towns came from local sources which helped keep many families afloat. There was usually a meat market, a creamery, a dairy, a candy company, and a bakery or two that made its own bread and donuts. Most blacksmiths had disappeared, but there were a lot more garages and parts companies.

Despite hard times and lean cash, thousands sought comic relief and forgetfulness at the movies. Oklahoma's Will Rogers — one of the biggest stars — roped man, mouse and horse but never kissed the girl with any precision. Fred Astaire and Ginger Rogers danced across the silver screen, while Shirley Temple tapped her way into America's hearts. Talkies were in, and some of the most stunning of the silent screen stars saw their careers dashed as they opened their mouths. Clara Bow's thick Brooklyn accent finished off her career.

46

*Flying High*
*Airplanes had been transformed from wartime battle to such uses as aerial geological reconnaissance and mail flights. Passengers were restricted to one, and the open-air cockpit usually limited flying to good weather.*
*Creek Council House.*

There were also real live heroes, such as Wiley Post, noted Oklahoma air pilot. Post completed the first solo round-the-world flight of 16,474 miles in eight days, 15 hours and 51 minutes. He also introduced "space suits" for his ventures into altitude testing.

Few people had money for furniture or luxuries, but they would spend for a family radio if they had any discretionary funds. A new Majestic radio "complete with tubes" was $44.50; a more expensive furniture model was $99.50. The cost was easy to justify when every evening an entire family could be entertained and informed. Nearly 14 million Americans owned radios. If you were willing to put up with a little static, there was plenty to choose from. There were 618 radio stations and networks broadcasting coast to coast. For the cultured listener, there was the Philco Hour, Chase & Sanborn's Orchestra, Firestone Orchestra, Soconyland Sketches, Old Gold's Paul Whiteman Orchestra and the Kellogg Radio Town Crier. On the more popular side, there was Little Orphan Annie and Sandy, Amos 'n' Andy, Buck Rogers, Flash Gordon and Jack Armstrong, the All-American Boy.

48

***Straight and Narrow***
*The Women's Christian Temperance Union was determined to eliminate alcohol and the consequences it visited upon families. They were always visible in parades and special events, such as this Parade of the Counties in 1932.*
*Oklahoma State Historical Society.*

# FIGHTING FEAR WITH FIRESIDE CHATS

In March 1933, the confident voice of newly-elected President Franklin D. Roosevelt wafted across the air waves and into the homes of Americans everywhere. His fireside chats were designed to give the country confidence and allay its growing fears. The country had every right to be afraid. All the banks had closed. Everyone hoped that his words would produce the confidence needed for good things to happen.

Roosevelt promised action — and he gave it. The New Deal included a host of government programs to reach out to the common people, particularly hard-pressed farmers. But Roosevelt was up against more than just a national panic — he was up against a regional drought of astronomical proportions. The land had dried out, and the overworked soil had given up. When the winds came, it was as if the land had abandoned its former home. It simply picked up and blew away. Families woke up to find crops, fields and fences half-buried with dry powdery soil blown from other farms in other states. There was no rain, no crops, no water and no food.

In the towns, churches and benevolent groups set up breadlines and soup kitchens to feed the hungry. Millions wandered aimlessly, looking for food or work. Men became door-to-door salesmen for whatever seemed saleable — pots and pans, encyclopedias, spices, Bibles. The young stayed in school because there were no jobs.

50

**Store-Bought Goods**
*Kellogg's, Cloverbloom, Star, Nabisco (Uneeda) were already household names in the grocery stores where canned and processed foods were growing more popular. This Sun Grocery in Henryetta later became Safeway. Joe Hardin/Mildred Hardin Collection.*

# DEPRESSION PRICES

1932-1935

| | | |
|---|---|---|
| Bacon | .22 | pound |
| Bread | .05 | 20 oz. |
| Butter | .19 | pound |
| Chicken | .22 | pound |
| Coffee | .26 | pound |
| Corn flakes | .01 | ounce |
| Eggs | .25 | 2 dozen |
| Flour | .99 | per 24.5 pounds of flour/ one pkg. cake flour |
| Ham | .31 | pound |
| Pork & beans | 1.00 | 20 large cans |
| Pork chops | .20 | pound |
| Potatoes | 1.35 | per 100 pounds |
| Round steak | .26 | pound |
| Sour cream | .09 | pound |
| Spring lamb chops | .24 | pound |
| Cigarettes | .25 | 2 packs |
| Carton | 1.17 | |
| Percolator | 1.39 | |
| Gas stove | 23.95 | |
| Shirt | .47 | |
| Dry clean | .19 | |

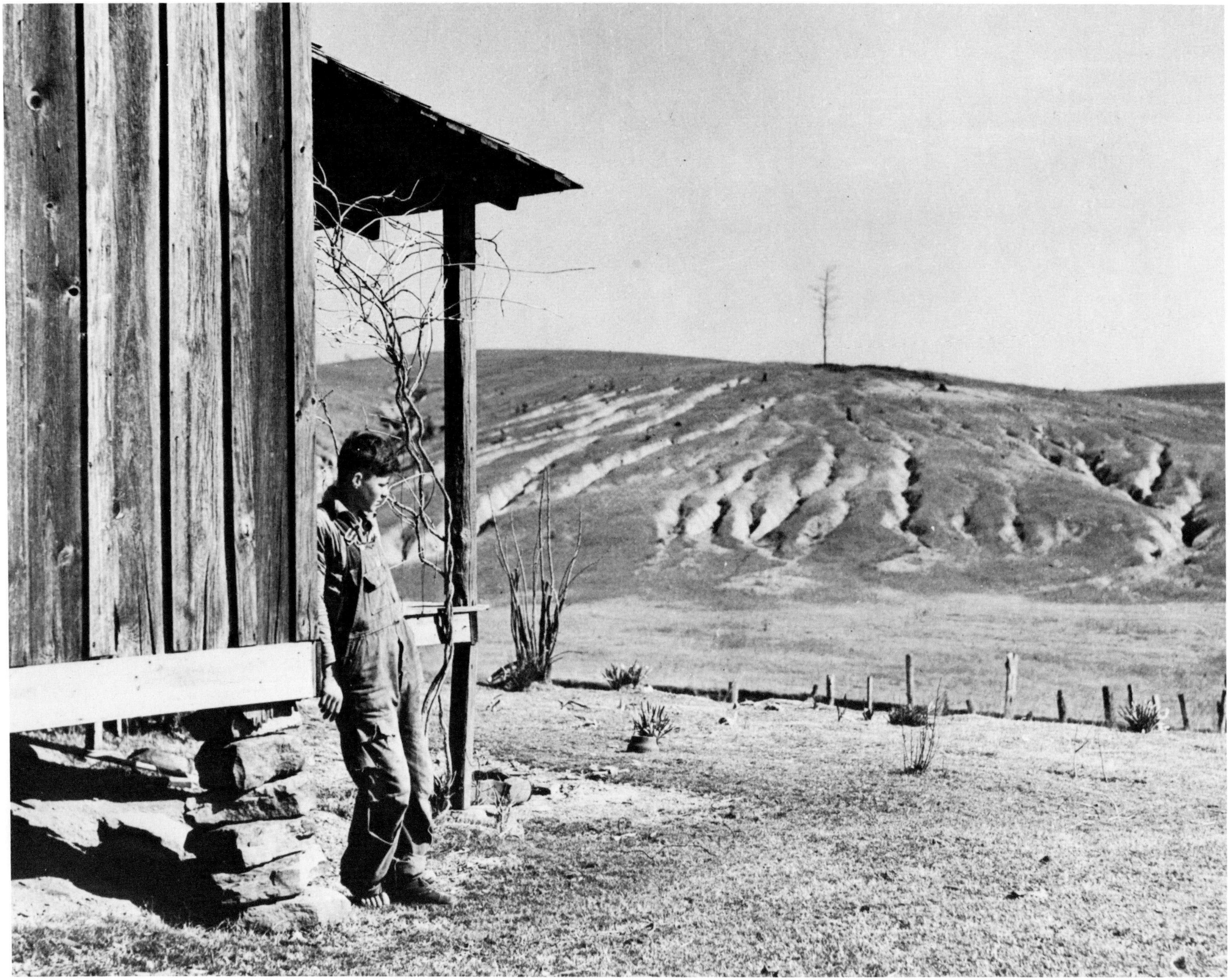

*No Sign of Rain*
*By the 1930s, Oklahomans found themselves in the worst drought that had ever been recorded. Coupled by troubled economic times and the stock market crash of 1929, many had to abandon homes and farms. When John Steinbeck chronicled the terrible ordeal of displaced Oklahomans in Grapes of Wrath, the book drew praise from literary critics and denunciations from those who could not believe that it was really that bad.*
*Library of Congress.*

Prices continued to drop. Corn was 10 cents a bushel. Crude oil was 25 cents a barrel. Even liquor went down when prohibition was repealed December 4, 1933. Oklahoma remained silent while other states rejoiced; it had not been one of the 19 states to ratify the act.

On New Year's Day, Capitol State Bank of Oklahoma City closed its doors for the holiday and decided to simply shut down business. The weather was on a rampage. All through the next year, it continued — hail, tornadoes, drought and dust. By summer, dust storms across the Midwest had destroyed crops and removed all the topsoil. When the rain came, it eroded the barren land. The newly-established Soil Conservation Service sought ways to improve farming methods. The Resettlement Administration helped farmers find new farms or low-income housing in the suburbs. The Works Progress Administration provided government aid and work for the unemployed. Men rebuilt bridges, roads and schoolhouses.

In 1935, oil man E.W. Marland was inaugurated as governor. A wildcat well near Edmond opened a new oil field and set off one more oil boom. A meeting of eight oil-producing states was held in Ponca City, laying the groundwork for the Interstate Oil and Gas Compact Commission. Will Rogers and Wiley Post died in Alaska when their plane crashed. The nation mourned two great Oklahomans.

54

*Riding the Rails*
*Those who had no transportation hit the rails, living in hobo jungles along the rivers and streams or wherever they could find a little shelter.*
*Blakey Group Collection.*

# Hard Travelin'

By summer, Oklahoma was declared a disaster area. The average temperature in August was 105.3 degrees. The Arkansas River running through Tulsa was so dry that the driftwood caught fire. A lot of Oklahomans — sharecroppers and farmers — saw no reason to stay and picked up what little possessions they had left, tied them to whatever vehicle was still running and headed west. There was work in California — or so they heard. Those who did not have an automobile, hopped a freight. But California was no garden of Eden. A surplus of workers drove wages to the basement, and families found themselves caught in a vicious cycle of abject poverty. Oklahoman Woody Guthrie traveled the California migrant camps and saw the hunger and desperation. He slept in jails with the cells piled high with young boys, strong men and old men that sung and talked hard-luck stories. His own songs chronicled a part of Oklahoma's history and America's national folklore.

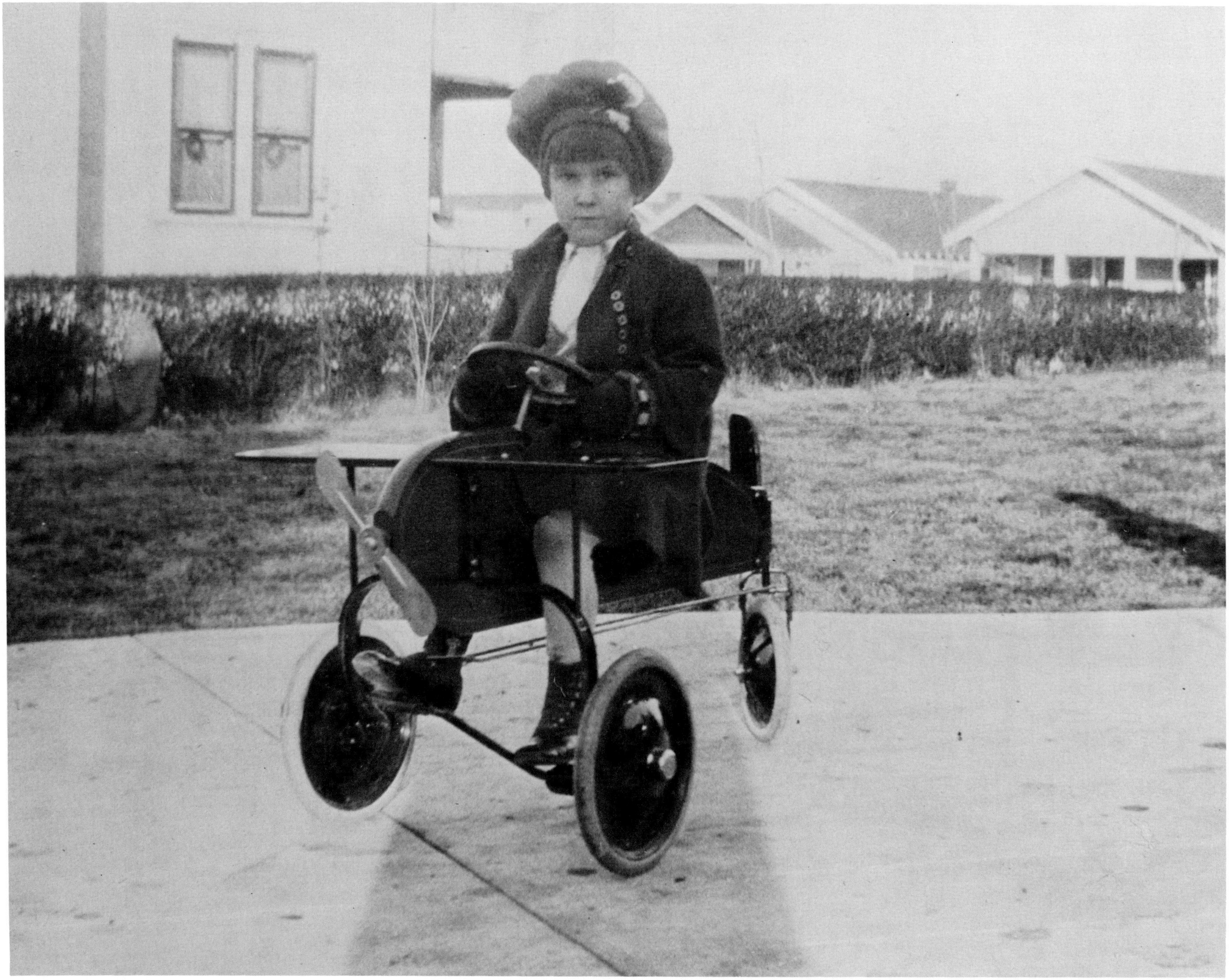

***Flight of Fancy***
*Children of those who had jobs or money in the larger towns played with Princess Elizabeth paper dolls and found fancy tricycles and wagons under their Christmas trees.*
*Beverly Jenkins/Blakey Group Collection.*

Between 1936 and 1940, 11 million Americans were unemployed. There were over 5,000 strikes as labor and management clashed. The First Annual Indian Exposition was held in Tulsa in October 1936. Construction was begun on the Grand River Dam in eastern Oklahoma the next year. *Gone with the Wind* was the blockbuster bestseller, and Mae West was famous for her "come up and see me sometime." Dale Carnegie published *How to Win Friends and Influence People*. The Social Security Act passed to help everyone "save toward his old age."

Charlie McCarthy was the big radio hero. Oklahoma's Tennessee Valley Boys played live over KVOO. KHBG in Okmulgee featured its own six-man band, the Western Swingsters.

Children made do with mud pies, wood scraps and other assorted throwaways for toys. Brown paper sacks made wonderful doll clothes or dress-up clothes although not as fancy as the Princess Elizabeth and Princess Margaret Rose paper cutouts in the dime store. A doll carriage was a cherished Christmas gift ($4.98) or a trike a truly splendid set of wheels ($3.98) — particularly sacrificial when a used '29 Ford could be had for $57.50 and a farmhand earned a mere $216 a year. Tuition at the University of Tulsa was $175 a year. A dental filling cost $1, and the receptionist who worked for the dentists might be paid $2 a week and lunch.

Lowering cylinder after completion of Blowing

58

***White-Hot Glass***
*Blacks and whites worked side by side in the glass plants, which manufactured everything from window glass to canning jars to automobile windows. Baker Brothers Glass workers lower a cylinder of glass after blowing has been completed.*
*Joe Hardin/Mildred Hardin Collection.*

Barter became a way of life. Town women supplemented family income by teaching piano lessons at 25 cents a lesson — if 25 cents were to be had. More often, it came out in quilt tops, permanent waves, a down payment on a piano or laundry. Farm boys hired out to do farm chores on neighboring farms if they had time to finish their own. Town boys worked their way through high school as paper carriers or as ushers in the fancy downtown theaters for 35 cents an hour. Good roughnecks earned 77 cents an hour, but not that many rigs were working.

Al Capone attempted to buy the Miller Brothers' 101 Ranch to convert it to a colony where Italian families could produce Italian food for American consumption to escape the high federal tariffs on imports. But the plan failed, and the ranch went on the auction block.

60

***The Hometown Team***
*Hometown sports were big events, and even the large companies had teams. The Cities Service team in Bartlesville had its own special uniforms and new equipment. Inter-company and inter-city competition was at an all-time high, and oil field camps spawned some almost-professional teams.*
*Cities Service Oil and Gas Corporation Collection.*

In 1938, Joe Louis knocked out Max Schmeling in the first round at Yankee Stadium. Orson Wells presented "War of the Worlds," the first "radio docudrama," on Halloween; thousands panicked when they thought earth had been invaded by beings from outer space. The Federal Communications Commission clamped a lid on experiments with television, fearing it might affect radio broadcasting.

The drought did not go away. Water witches sought underground water with peach tree limbs. Farmers who still had a sense of humor joked that they got a half day's relief between spring and summer dust storms, and a day and a half between summer and fall ones. Others sighed and remarked that they hoped it would rain before the kids grew up because the children had never seen water fall from the sky. The only good thing on the farm seemed to be the new Rural Electrification Act which brought electricity and revolutionized farm life.

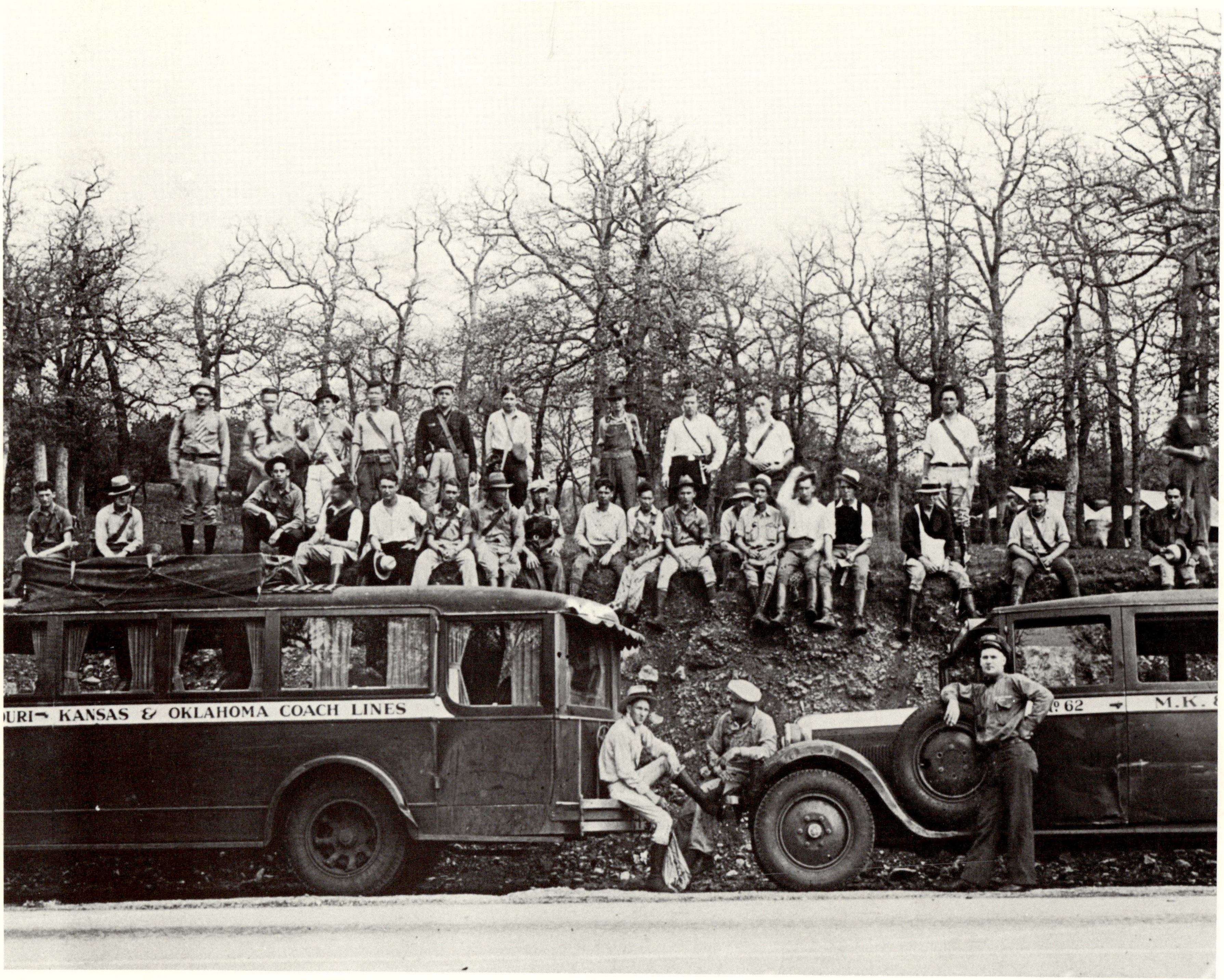
OURI— KANSAS & OKLAHOMA COACH LINES
Nº 62
M.K. &

*Geology 303*
*Oil was being found by a new breed of oil man — the geologist, and hundreds of men took training in how to trek through a field and figure out what lay beneath. You could always spot a geologist: he was the one with pants tucked inside high boots. There was good reason for the practice. Any experienced field man knew it discouraged chiggers, scorpions and other assorted varmints.*
*Special Collections, McFarlin Library, University of Tulsa.*

Suddenly, the world was preoccupied by the familiar spectre of war. Radio brought Hitler into American homes, and hostility toward German leaders grew. Czechoslovakia fell to German forces early in 1939 and Poland later that year. The *Tulsa World* assured Oklahomans in an editorial that the United States would not enter the war. In June, Hitler took Paris. America cringed at getting involved once again. Still, it could not turn its back completely. Cities held aluminum drives and prepared to gear up to help American allies. Factories began to whir again. There were jobs once more. Wages went up, and so did prices. No one seemed to mind too much. Families had roofs over their heads, and the children went to bed with full stomachs and smiles. It was the paradox of an industrial economy: there was war on the horizon, but there was hope in America's eyes.

*Oklahoma Writers Project/Oklahoma State Historical Society*

*A Special Thanks...*
*In 1919, Joe Hardin moved to Henryetta and set up a studio in the Perry Building. For 49 years, he chronicled the growth of small-town Oklahoma — its people at work and at play. He served as official photographer for the Frisco Railroad in the area and for Governor William Murray. He died in his studio in 1968. His daughter, Mildred Hardin Walker, has preserved his work and shared it with the Oklahoma community for the last 15 years.*

**Acknowledgements**

**Photographs have been provided courtesy of the following museums and collections:**

**Blakey Group Collection**
**Cities Services Oil and Gas Corp. Collection**
**Beryl Ford Collection**
**Mildred Hardin Collection**
**Beverly Jenkins**
**Library of Congress**
**Oklahoma State Historical Society**
**Okmulgee Public Library**
**Tulsa Chamber of Commerce**
**The University of Tulsa, McFarlin Library Collection**
**Creek Council House**

**Copyright 1984 by Ellen Sue Blakey**
**All rights reserved**

**Concept and design: The Blakey Group Inc, Tulsa, Oklahoma**